DASH Diet Smoothies

100 Nutrition Packed Smoothies for Weight Loss

By Renee Sanders

DASH Diet Smoothies

Published by Awesome Life Resources. 2015

Ebook ASIN: B00T82UAEM

Paperback ISBN: 978-1508657415

Table of Contents

Berry banana buttermilk smoothie

Blue Razzy smoothie

Beery oats low calorie smoothie

Powerful pomegranate smoothie

Raspberry oats smoothie

Porridge berry smoothie

Banana Pinkberry smoothie

Blueberry white milk smoothie

Avocado berry spinach smoothie

Four berries smoothie

Green Smoothies

Spinach super green smoothie

Super Morning smoothie

Happiness green smoothie

Green peach smoothie

Coconut milk debloating smoothie

Goddess green happiness smoothie

Lucky beginner's smoothie

Banana protein spinach smoothie

Fresh Kale & banana smoothie

Twisty Kiwi smoothie

Yogurt Smoothies

Mixy groovie smoothie

Sunshine Orange smoothie

Breakfast berry smoothie

Summer sweet smoothie

Berry yogurt healthy smoothie

Fruity juicy smoothie

White coconut milk smoothie

Red apple yogurt smoothie

Frozen strawberry yogurt smoothie

Simply protein green smoothie

Frozen blu-yogurt smoothie

Gold peach smoothie

Fruity Oaty yogurt smoothie

Juicy Ma-Ba smoothie

Super sunshine Fruity smoothie

Sleepy berry yogurt smoothie

Coconut fruity smoothie

Yogy-fruity smoothie

Healthy fruity oats smoothie

Peachy mango smoothie

Fruit Smoothies

Tropical fruity cilantro smoothie

Super mango honey smoothie

Chocky banana smoothie

Gingery peach smoothie

Banana cherry smoothie

Appy fruity smoothie

Fruity nutty smoothie

Gold nectar smoothie

Creamy peachy smoothie

Mango papaya smoothie

Vegetable Smoothies

Cucumber strawberry smoothie

Bloody mary spicy smoothie

Pumpkin low-carb smoothie

Purple smoothie

Spring smoothie

Superbly soy smoothie

Golden carrot smoothie

Spicy pumpkin smoothie

Harvest smoothie

Pumpkin pie smoothie

Superfood Smoothies

Lemonade Aloe Vera smoothie

Bee Pollen Blissful smoothie

Gingerly Butter chocolate smoothie

Chlorella Pineapple smoothie

Super energizer coconut smoothie

Gelatin T-mac smoothie

Goji-Raspy smoothie

Hemp brain booster smoothie

Marvelous maca smoothie

Colostrums chocolate smoothie

Nuts & Seeds Smoothies

Chunky monkey smoothie

Almond berry butter smoothie

FREE BONUS!

To help you start your DASH diet and stay committed to your diet plan, I've put together a DASH Diet Hamper which includes the following:

    a. Audio version of the Amazon Bestseller book **"Blood Pressure Solution" by Jessica Robbins**
    b. **7 day vegetarian meal plan** for DASH Diet
    c. DASH Diet Shopping List
    d. Tips to get started with the DASH Diet
    e. Tips to reduce your sodium intake
    f. Sodium Content Chart of various foods

<u>Additional Bonus!</u>

Receive the first copies of all my diet and cookbooks as soon as they get published for FREE!

Get Access to the FREE DASH Diet Hamper, by clicking HERE: http://dietcookbooks.co/dashdiet/

Introduction

Thank you for downloading my book DASH Diet Smoothies: 100 Nutrition Packed Smoothies for Weight Loss.

Most of us stroll into our kitchens rather wobbly first thing in the morning, and reach for a cup of coffee or tea for a morning kick. Instead of starting your day with a caffeinated bump, consider sipping something a little more refreshing and nourishing. These juice and smoothie recipes are as good for you as they are delicious, and can be enjoyed as either a wake-up jolt or for a rejuvenating afternoon. Fresh nutrients and enzymes in juices and smoothies not only feed every cell in your body but also keep you hydrated from the fruits. Now, that's a far better method of staying awake and energetic than knocking back all those dehydrating caffeine drinks

In this book, I've carefully handpicked 100 smoothies from among the thousands of recipes in my kitchen diary. All the recipes in this book adhere to the recommendations prescribed by the DASH diet. This diet mainly focuses on how to keep your blood pressure under control by eating low sodium based foods. As this diet promotes healthy eating, people without high blood pressure also follow it because of the numerous benefits it offers like weight reduction and protection against diabetes, cancer, osteoporosis, cardiovascular diseases, stroke etc.

For the 5th year in a row, DASH Diet has been ranked as the #1 diet among the 35 diets evaluated and ranked by US News & World Report. According to the experts in their panel, "To be top-rated, a diet has to be relatively easy to follow, nutritious, safe and effective for weight loss and against diabetes and heart disease". Studies sponsored by the National Heart, Lung, and Blood Institute (NHLBI) have proven that DASH diet reduces high blood pressure, which in turn lowers the risk of developing cardiovascular disease.

What is DASH diet?

This chapter is taken from my <u>DASH Diet for Vegetarians</u> book.

The DASH (Dietary Approach to Stop Hypertension) diet is prescribed as the best diet to lower the blood pressure by eating less sodium. Apart from avoiding sodium, the main key ingredients that are involved in this diet are foods rich in potassium, calcium and magnesium which are connected to lowering blood pressure. This dietary goal can be achieved by combining fresh fruits and vegetables, low fat and non-fat dairy products, nuts, legumes and whole grains in the daily diet. Additionally, DASH diet helps in reducing cholesterol, which in turn helps in weight loss and reduces the risk of heart strokes, osteoporosis, several types of cancer, kidney stones and diabetes.

Guidelines to be followed while dash dieting.

No Special foods

Unlike other diet plans, DASH diet is very easy to follow as it does not suggest any special foods to be consumed. By making small changes to your normal diet and the cooking methods, you can easily follow the guidelines of this diet.

Foods to be included

Vegetable and fruit consumption has to be increased, especially lot of dark-green vegetables, tomatoes, beans, carrots, broccoli and peas – at least 4-5 servings per day. Examples: apricots, bananas, dates, grapes, oranges, grapefruit, mangoes, melons, peaches, pineapples, prunes, strawberries, tangerines

Refined grains have to be totally replaced and whole grains should be taken as whole grains contain more fiber and are packed with nutrients – 6-8 servings per day.

Low fat & non fat dairy products like skimmed milk, buttermilk and fat free yogurt can be consumed- 2-3 servings per day.

4-5 servings per day of nuts and seeds like peanuts, walnuts, sunflower seeds, almonds etc are beneficial.

Lean meats like skinless chicken, sea foods etc. can be consumed. Vegetarians can opt for other plant-based sources of protein like soy and tofu.

Food to be avoided

It is advised to reduce the food consumption of refined food grains that contain fats, added sugars and salts (sodium).

Red meats, aerated sugary beverages and sweets like jelly, jam, sorbet, maple syrup etc. should be avoided- not more than 5 servings per week.

Do not consume more than 2-3 servings of oils and fats per day. This includes the oil used for cooking, salad dressing, sandwich spreads etc. Avoid unsaturated fats and transfats as much as possible.

Alcohol consumption should be restricted. Men shouldn't take more than 2 servings of alcohol per day and women shouldn't consume more than 1 serving per day.

Balance the calories with exercise to manage weight

Try to reduce weight if you are overweight or obese and maintain a healthy weight by a constant improvement in eating healthy food and also by involving in various physical activities. The American Heart Association recommends 30 minutes of exercise per day, 5 times week, in addition to following the diet plan.

It's also advised to balance your calorie intake depending on the stage of your life cycle – E.g. pregnancy, older age etc. and the type of your lifestyle- sedentary, moderate or active.

DASH Diet Aim

The DASH (Dietary Approaches to Stop Hypertension) eating plan is recommended to help lower blood pressure by the National Institutes of Health and most physicians. The DASH diet is rich in fruits, vegetables, low fat or non-fat dairy, and also includes grains, especially whole grains; lean meats, fish and poultry; nuts and beans. In addition to lowering blood pressure, it has been shown to lower cholesterol. It is an extremely healthy way of eating, designed to be flexible enough to meet the lifestyle and food preferences of most people.

DASH diet: Sodium levels

Standard DASH diet - You can consume up to 2,300 milligrams (mg) of sodium a day.

Lower sodium DASH diet - You can consume up to 1,500 mg of sodium a day.

Both versions of the DASH diet aim to reduce the amount of sodium in your diet compared with what you might get in a more traditional diet, which can amount to a whopping 3,500 mg of sodium a day or more.

The standard DASH diet meets the recommendation from the Dietary Guidelines for Americans to keep daily sodium intake to less than 2,300 mg a day. The lower sodium version of the diet matches the recommendation to reduce sodium to 1,500 mg a day if you're 51 and older, black, or have hypertension, diabetes or chronic kidney disease. The American Heart Association recommends 1,500 mg as an upper limit for all adults. If you aren't sure what sodium level is right for you, it is best to consult your doctor.

DASH diet recommendations for a 2000 Calorie Diet plan would be as follows:

Total fat	27% of calories
Saturated fat	6% of calories
Protein	18% of calories
Carbohydrate	55% of calories
Cholesterol	150 mg
Sodium	2,300 mg*
Potassium	4,700 mg
Calcium	1,250 mg
Magnesium	500 mg
Fiber	30 g

An easier way to track your diet would be to keep a check on the number of servings of each food group. Here is the DASH diet recommendation for a 1600 cal/day and a 2000 cal/day diet plan.

	Servings per Day	
Food Group	**1600 Calories**	**2000 Calories**
Grains & Grain Products	6	7-8
Vegetables	3-4	4-5
Fruits	4	4-5
Low Fat or Fat-free Dairy Foods	2-3	2-3
Meats/ poultry/ fish/	1-2	2 or less

vegetarian alternatives		
Nuts, seeds, dry beans	3 per week	4-5 per week
Fast & oils	2	2-3
Sweets	2 per week	5 per week

Sodium Intake & Weight Loss Connection

Why is DASH Diet so good for weight loss? Salt plays a key role in weight gain. As DASH Diet is low on sodium, it automatically leads to weight loss. The connection between sodium intake and weight loss can be explained this way:

When you consume salty foods, your body tends to retain more water. To maintain the water balance due to increased intake of sodium, you excrete less urine. As a result your body looks more bloated and your face looks puffier. This is also known as water weight.

Eating salty food also makes you instantly thirsty. Most people drink packaged beverages that are loaded with sugars to quench this thirst. This leads to higher intake of calories, which in turn leads to obesity. This is probably why most fast food restaurants sell these sugary drinks in plenty.

We must agree that adding more salt makes the food taste yummier. This is another reason why we tend to eat more when the food is salty.

In the following chapters let's see some delicious and easy to prepare smoothies that are low in sodium as per the DASH diet guidelines. If you hate eating fruits and veggies, then this book would be a delight as you can have your recommended 4-5 servings of fruits and vegetables in the form of these tasty smoothies.

Smoothie Recipes: The Basics First

What are smoothies?

Smoothies are blended drinks made from various combinations of fruits, fruit juices, yogurt, nuts and spices and ice cubes. They are alternatives to fat filled milkshakes. They derived their name from the smooth texture of the emulsion. Traditional ones sold in the United States are relatively free of dairy products, relying on fruits such as bananas to provide thickness and sweetness. Smoothies produced in other countries often contain yogurt as a thickener and honey as a natural sweetener.

What you'll need: a juicer, a blender or food processor, fresh fruits and vegetables, milk, herbs, and spices as the recipes require.

Smoothies can make you full, satisfying your crave for sweet and when made the right way, provide you with loads of proteins and vitamins. They're great in the morning to kick start your day. Many smoothie makers try to make smoothies by adding extra sweeteners and extra calories to make their mixture irresistible. However, to obtain the nutritional benefits and spare your waistline, follow our steps to perfect your perfect smoothie concoctions.

What are the advantages of smoothies?

- It's always quick and easy to make.
- It can be replaced as a meal or a snack depending on the calories one should consume as per your diet.
- It can be specifically made to target your nutritional needs keeping in the calorie count.
- It's a booster for weight and fast loss
- Helps or aids in muscle growth
- It's a natural drink made with nutrient and enzymes that can help your body to keep hydrated always.
- It helps in controlling blood sugar levels.
- It helps in decreasing the stress hormones and keeps you rejuvenated.
- It strengthens bones.

Components of a basic smoothie

1) Liquid

Liquid is necessary to blend your smoothie and add consistency. Start with 1/4 cup. If your smoothie doesn't mix when the blender is turned on, add more liquid. You can choose to use filtered water, milk (almond, skim, soya, rice or coconut) to add calcium, coconut nut water for a tropical flavor, fresh fruit juice without any sweeteners and green tea.

2) Fruit

You can use combination or fresh or frozen fruits as per the recipe. Fruit provides plenty of options and the combinations are endless: strawberry, blueberry, pineapple, blackberry, raspberry, mango, peach, pear, orange, banana and so on.

3) Thickening agent

If you want your smoothie to be thick, you can always add ice cubes at the first step. If you want it thicker, banana is a thickening agent that can be used or try some more extra frozen fruits. Another agent that be used is yogurt which gives a nice texture. Greek yogurt, low-fat frozen yogurt, avocado, peanut butternut and soft tofu are great other alternatives.

4) Extra Flavor

Depending on the sweetness of the fruit or the freshness you may want to add some extra flavor to the smoothie. Always avoid adding extra sweeteners to it. Instead of adding extra sweeteners, you can add vanilla extract, honey, agave nectar, dates etc. Add some herbs & spices like cinnamon, nutmeg, allspice, cloves, cardamom, vanilla, mint, cilantro etc. for an extra flavor which will add a natural healthy flavor to the drink.

Additional tips to make a healthy smoothie

Try using an overripe banana to get the nice texture and natural sweetness to the smoothie. These brown overripe bananas can also be frozen and used as a source of sweetness.

To get a creamy texture to the smoothie, try using bananas, papaya, mango, peach, etc. which are categorized as creamy fruits and always add water rich fruits mildly to avoid a watery drink like citrus fruits, watermelons etc.

Sticking to only water, fruit and ice will make your smoothie with fewer calories.

If the smoothie turns out bitter, you can always make it better by adding a sweet fruit like dates, pineapples, berries or overripe bananas.

Always try having your smoothies fresh, whenever you are ready to have it. Don't allow it to sit for too long as the nutrients in the smoothies will be lost.

Berry Smoothies

Fruit Salad smoothie

Serving-2, Duration- 10min

Ingredients

1 banana (ripe, sliced)

1 cup strawberries (sliced, chilled)

1 cup pineapple (cubed, chilled)

1 cup orange juice

1/2 lime

1 tbsp honey

Directions

Blend the banana, strawberries, pineapple, orange juice, lime, and honey in a blender. Process until smooth. Pour into glasses and serve immediately.

Simply Strawberry smoothie

Servings- 2, Duration- 5minutes

Ingredients

3 cups frozen strawberries

1 1/2 cups milk (any variety)

1/3 cup strawberry jam

Directions

Combine the frozen strawberries, strawberry jam and milk in the blender. Puree until smooth and serve immediately.

Super Fruit Healthy smoothie

Servings-2, Duration- 10min

Ingredients

1/3 cup fresh blueberries

1/3 cup fresh raspberries

4 strawberries (large fresh)

1/3 cup pomegranate juice

1/3 cup mango juice

2/3 cup milk

2 tsp honey

Directions

Combine the blueberries, raspberries, strawberries, pomegranate and mango juices, milk, and honey into a blender. Cover, and puree until smooth. Pour into glasses to serve immediately.

Soy Strawberry smoothie

Servings- 2, Duration-10minutes

Ingredients

1 banana (ripe, sliced)

2 cups strawberries

1 cup soy milk

2 tsp honey

Directions

Take a blender, combine ripe banana, strawberries, soy milk, and honey. Puree until smooth. Serve immediately.

Blueberry Fruit smoothie

Servings-1, Duration-10minutes

Ingredients

1/2 cup frozen blueberries

1/4 cup cranberry juice (unsweetened)

2 bananas

Directions

In a blender, blend all the ingredients until smoothie and serve immediately.

Red Fruit smoothie

Servings- 4, Durations- 15minutes

Ingredients

2 orange peels (cut in chunks and pith removed)

1 cup raspberries (frozen)

1 cup frozen blueberries

Directions

Take a blender; puree all the ingredients in a blender until smooth. Serve immediately.

Detox Berry smoothie

Servings- 4, Durations-10minutes

Ingredients

6 bananas (5 frozen for frothy consistency)

1/2 cup blueberries (frozen if not in season)

1/4 cup strawberries (frozen if not in season)

1/4 cup raspberries

16 ozs cold water (filtered)

Directions

Combine and blend all the ingredients together in the blender until you have a smooth and creamy consistency.

Straw-Blue smoothie

Servings- 4, Durations- 10minutes

Ingredients

1 cup frozen strawberries

1/2 cup frozen blueberries

1 cup milk

Directions

Combine all ingredients in a blender then blend until smooth. Pour in a glass and serve immediately. Enjoy!

Coconut Water Pink smoothie

Servings- 1, Duration- 15minutes

Ingredients

3/4 cup frozen strawberries

1 cup coconut water

Directions

Take a blender; puree both the ingredients until smoothie and serve immediately.

Cherry- Berry Fruity smoothie

Servings- 4, Duration- 15minutes

Ingredients

2 cups orange juice

2 bananas

2 cups frozen blueberries

1 cup cherries (frozen)

Directions

Take a blender, combine all ingredients as listed and blend it until smooth and enjoy!!!

Berry banana buttermilk smoothie

Servings-3, Duration- 10minutes

Ingredients

2 cups blueberries (frozen)

1 bananas (peeled and cubed)

11/2 cups buttermilk

31/2 tsp agave nectar

1/4 tsp cinnamon

Directions

Combine all ingredients into a blender in the order listed. Blend until smooth or desired consistency has been achieved .Serve immediately.

Blue Razzy smoothie

Servings-3, Duration-10 minutes

Ingredients

1 banana

16 whole almonds

1/4 cup rolled oats

1 tbsp flax seed meal

1 cup frozen blueberries

1 cup yogurt (raspberry)

1/4 cup grape juice (Concord)

1 cup buttermilk

Directions

Freeze the cut bananas for about 2hrs. Place the almonds, oats, and flaxseed meal into a blender; pulse until finely ground. Add the frozen banana, frozen blueberries, yogurt, grape juice, and buttermilk; puree until smooth. Serve chilled immediately.

Beery oats low calorie smoothie

Servings-2, Duration- 10mts

Ingredients

1/3 cup frozen blueberries

1/3 cup frozen raspberries

1/3 cup frozen blackberries

1/4 cup instant oatmeal

1 cup almond milk (or vanilla almond)

2 tsp honey (or agave nectar)

1 tsp orange zest

Directions

In a blender, combine milk and instant oats, blend until smooth. Add blueberries, blackberries and raspberries and blend for 20 seconds. If mixture is too thick, add a little more milk. Atlast, add honey and orange zest.

Powerful pomegranate smoothie

Servings- 1, Duration-20minutes

Ingredients

1 cup unsweetened pomegranate juice

1 decent handful organic baby spinach

1 handful frozen mangoes

1 handful organic frozen blueberries

2 tsp oatmeal

1 whole orange (peeled and chopped)

Directions

Place all ingredients into your blender and blend to desired smoothness. Pour into glasses, garnish with a few pomegranate arils and serve immediately.

Raspberry oats smoothie

Servings-1, Duration-3minutes

Ingredients

1 1/2 tablespoons oatmeal

1 cup raspberries

2 teaspoons honey

1/2 cup water

3 teaspoons plain yogurt

Directions

Boil oats in boiling water for 10minutes. Put the soaked oats in the blender and all remaining ingredients, reserving 1 tsp of yogurt. Blend until smooth. Pour the smoothie into a glass. Swirl in reserved yogurt and garnish with a few additional raspberries if desired.

Porridge berry smoothie

Servings-1, Duration-20 minutes

Ingredients

25 grams porridge oats

300 ml low-fat milk

100 grams plain yogurt

50 grams blueberries

50 grams strawberries (roughly chopped)

Directions

Combine the oats and milk in a small saucepan, bring to the boil and simmer for 2 minutes. Transfer the porridge to a liquidizer or food processor, add the remaining ingredients and blend until smooth. Serve while still warm.

Banana Pinkberry smoothie

Servings-4, Duration-15mts

Ingredients

11/2 cups frozen strawberries

1 banana

2 orange (medium sized)

2 cups ice

1 tbsp honey

Directions

Combine the strawberries, banana and ice to the blender. Squeeze the oranges into the blender, add honey and Serve immediately.

Blueberry white milk smoothie

Servings-2, Duration-10mts

Ingredients

1/4 cup coconut milk (canned)

1/2 cup water

1 banana

1 cup frozen blueberries

1 tbsp raw almond

Directions

Place coconut milk, water, banana, blueberries and almonds to blender container. Cover and blend until smooth. Pour into 2 glasses and serve immediately.

Avocado berry spinach smoothie

Servings-1, Duration-5mts

Ingredients

1 cup blueberries

1 cup fresh spinach

1 cup coconut milk

1/2 avocado (skinned and ripe)

1 tbsp Chia seeds

1/4 tsp cinnamon

1 tbsp honey

1 scoop protein powder

1/2 ice (fresh)

Directions

Place all ingredients in blender and puree. Serve in glass. Add a few fresh blueberries and serve immediately.

Four berries smoothie

Servings-5, Duration-25mts

Ingredients

2 cups vanilla ice cream

1 cup frozen strawberries

3/4 cup frozen blueberries

1/2 cup raspberries

2 tsp sugar

1/2 cup cranberry juice

1 tbsp lemon juice

Fresh blueberries

Mint sprigs

Raspberries

Directions

Combine all the ingredients in the blender except the ice cubes and blend until smooth. Then add the ice cubes and blend it again to the desired smoothie consistency. Serve immediately.

Green Smoothies

Spinach super green smoothie

Servings- 1, Duration- 10minutes

Ingredients

1 banana (ripe and frozen)

1 spinach bunch (big heaping cup cleaned)

1 tbsp honey

1 tbsp greens (amazing grass, powder)

1 cup almond milk (cold)

Directions

Combine all the ingredients in a blender until smooth and serve immediately for a healthy drink.

Super Morning smoothie

Serving-1, Duration- 10minutes

Ingredients

1 handful kale (chopped spinach, collards or combination)

1 peeled banana

1 cup coconut water (pure unsweetened)

2 tsp almond butter

1 tbsp flaxseed oil

1/8 tsp ground cinnamon

Directions

Combine all ingredients in a blender and puree until completely blended and smoothened. Serve immediately.

Happiness green smoothie

Servings- 4, Duration- 5minutes

Ingredients

2 cups vanilla rice milk

4 cups fresh spinach

2 bananas (ripe)

1 tbsp agave nectar (or honey, or to taste)

Directions

Combine all the ingredients in a blender and purée until smooth. Divide among 4 glasses. If desired, serve with straws.

Green peach smoothie

Servings- 2, Duration- 20minutes

Ingredients

2 cups frozen peaches

2 handfuls of spinach

1 fresh peach, pitted and chopped (optional)

1 cup water

1 tablespoon peeled, minced or grated fresh ginger

1 tablespoon honey + more to taste

Directions

Take a blender and blend the frozen peaches, spinach, peach, water, and ginger until very smooth and add ¼ cup water if needed to keep the mixture moving smoothly through the blender. Add the honey, blend, and taste. Adjust the taste of the smoothie by adding, if necessary, ginger or honey and serve immediately.

Coconut milk debloating smoothie

Servings- 4, Duration- 5minutes

Ingredients

½ a medium banana, frozen

1 cup strawberries, frozen

1 cup pineapple, frozen

1 handful spinach, fresh

1 1/4 cups coconut milk from uncanned carton

Directions

Blend everything in the blender and until smooth. Serve immediately to enjoy!!!

Goddess green happiness smoothie

Servings- 4, Durations- 10minutes

Ingredients

2 green apples

1 banana

1 cup water

1 handful baby spinach

1/4 lime

Directions

Roughly cut the peeled apples. Wash the spinach. Add the chopped and peeled banana and squeeze quarter of lime to it. Combine all these in the blender and blend it until smooth and enjoy your smoothie!!!!

Lucky beginner's smoothie

Servings- 2, Durations- 15minutes

Ingredients

2 cups spinach, fresh (tightly packed)

2 cups water

1 cup mango

1 cup pineapple

2 bananas

Directions

Take the clean and washed spinach and add water and blend together until all leafy chunks are gone. Next add in mango, pineapple and bananas and blend again.

Banana protein spinach smoothie

Serving-4, Duration- 15minutes

Ingredients

1 tbsp almond butter

2/3 cup Greek yogurt

1/2 bananas

3/4 cup water

1 scoop vanilla protein

1 handful spinach

Directions

Take a blender, add all ingredients and blend it until smoothie texture. Serve and enjoy!!!

Fresh Kale & banana smoothie

Servings-1, Duration- 5minutes

Ingredients

1 banana

2 cups kale (chopped)

1/2 cup unsweetened soymilk (light)

1 tbsp flax seeds

1 tsp maple syrup

Directions

Combine all ingredients in a blender and blend until smooth and serve it immediately with ice cubes.

Twisty Kiwi smoothie

Servings-4, Duration-10minutes

Ingredients:

5-6 kiwis, sliced and frozen

2 large bananas, sliced and frozen

1 handful of fresh spinach

1 cup (240 g) Greek yogurt

½ cup (120 ml) milk

Directions

Blend kiwi, spinach and half of the milk until smooth, Pour into glasses, and then blend the banana slices with the yogurt and the remaining milk. Pour into glasses and serve immediately.

Yogurt Smoothies

Mixy groovie smoothie

Servings- 2, Duration-5minutes

Ingredients

2 bananas chunks

1 cup strawberries (frozen unsweetened)

8 ozs low-fat vanilla yogurt

3/4 cup milk

Directions

Take a blender and combine all ingredients and blend until smoothie and serve immediately.

Sunshine Orange smoothie

Servings-4, Duration-15minutes

Ingredients

2 whole orange (peeled)

1 handful mango (frozen, chunks)

1 container yogurt (vanilla bean)

1/2 bananas (frozen)

1 tbsp water (if necessary)

Directions

Combine all ingredients into your blender and blend until smooth, adding a few tablespoons of water if the smoothie becomes too thick. Enjoy!!!!!

Breakfast berry smoothie

Servings-4, Duration- 10minutes

Ingredients

1 cup frozen fruit

1/2 cup milk

1/2 cup yogurt (I use vanilla yogurt)

1 banana

Plain yogurt

Directions

Blend all the ingredients until smooth and serve immediately.

Summer sweet smoothie

Servings- 10, Duration-10minutes

Ingredients

1 cup vanilla yogurt

1/2 cup frozen strawberries

1/2 cup frozen peach slices

1/2 bananas (medium, peeled)

1/2 cup low-fat milk

Directions

Combine all ingredients in a blender; process until smooth and serve immediately.

Berry yogurt healthy smoothie

Servings-5, Durations- 5minutes

Ingredients

3/4 cup fresh blueberries

3/4 cup blackberries (fresh)

51/3 ozs Greek yogurt (package)

1 cup vanilla soy milk

1 whole banana

Directions

Take a blender, place all the ingredients in the blender and blend it well until smooth and serve immediately.

Fruity juicy smoothie

Serving- 2, Duration-10minutes

Ingredients

1 cup juice

11/2 cups yogurt

2 cups fruit (frozen)

Directions

Place all the ingredients in the blender and blend until smooth and serve immediately.

White coconut milk smoothie

Servings- 4, Duration- 15minutes

Ingredients

10 ozs frozen blueberries (or other fruit)

3 bananas (ripe)

1 cup plain yogurt

1 cup unsweetened coconut milk

2 tsp honey

Directions

Take a blender and blend all the ingredients and enjoy the smoothie by serving immediately!!!!

Red apple yogurt smoothie

Servings- 4, Duration-10minutes

Ingredients

5 raw almonds

1 red apple

1 banana

3/4 cup non-fat Greek yogurt

1/2 cup non-fat milk

1/4 tsp cinnamon

Directions

Combine all the ingredients in the blender and blend until smooth and serve immediately.

Frozen strawberry yogurt smoothie

Servings- 4, Duration- 10minutes

Ingredients

11/2 cups fat free milk

11/2 tsp strawberries

1 cup low-fat vanilla yogurt

1 cup frozen strawberries

Directions

Blend all the above ingredients in a blend until smoothie texture and serve immediately.

Simply protein green smoothie

Servings- 4, Durations- 10minutes

Ingredients

2 cups baby spinach

1 cup water

11/2 cups pineapple chunks (frozen)

1/2 bananas (small, frozen)

1/2 cup Greek yogurt

2 tsp honey

Directions

Take a blender and puree spinach and water in a high-power blender. Add frozen fruit, yogurt and honey and blend until smooth. Serve immediately.

Frozen blu-yogurt smoothie

Servings-4, Durations- 15minutes

Ingredients

1 cup fat free milk

1/4 cup orange juice

2 tsp vanilla yogurt

1 tbsp honey

1 banana

2/3 cup frozen blueberries

1/2 cup mango (chopped peeled, frozen)

11/4 cups peaches (frozen unsweetened sliced)

Directions

Take a blender and combine all the ingredients and blend it until smooth and serve chilled immediately.

Gold peach smoothie

Servings- 6, Duration- 10minutes

Ingredients

2 cups fresh orange juice

1 cup yogurt (peach)

2 cups peaches (frozen sliced)

2 tsp honey

1/4 tsp ground nutmeg

Directions

Take a blender, place all the above ingredients and blend it until smooth and serve immediately.

Fruity Oaty yogurt smoothie

Servings-2, Duration- 5minutes

Ingredients

1/2 cup coconut milk

1/2 cup pineapple chunks (frozen)

5 ozs Greek yogurt

1/4 cup oats

1/2 bananas

Directions

Take a blender and process the oats till it is powered and then add the remaining ingredients and blend together until smooth and serve chilled immediately.

Juicy Ma-Ba smoothie

Servings- 2, Duration- 5minutes

Ingredients

1 banana

1/2 cup mango (frozen, pieces)

1/3 cup plain yogurt

1/2 cup mango juice (orange-, blend)

Directions

Blend all the ingredients together until smooth and serve chilled immediately.

Super sunshine Fruity smoothie

Servings- 2, Duration- 5minutes

Ingredients

1 cup cold milk

2 orange (peeled and segmented)

1 banana

1/4 cup sugar

1 pinch salt

4 ozs fat free yogurt (vanilla)

4 cubes ice

Directions

Firstly place all the ingredients except the ice cubes and blend it until smooth and then add the ice cubes and blend it again and serve chilled.

Sleepy berry yogurt smoothie

Servings-4, Durations-10minutes

Ingredients

1 cup non-fat Greek yogurt

11/4 cups blueberries (plus more for garnish)

1/2 cup non-fat milk

1 tbsp honey

1/4 tsp ground cinnamon

1/8 tsp pure vanilla extract

Directions

Combine all the ingredients in a blender and blend until smooth and well-combined and serve immediately by garnishing it with blueberries.

Coconut fruity smoothie

Coconut fruity smoothie

Servings- 1, Duration- 10minutes

Ingredients

2 orange

1 banana

1/3 cup pineapple

1/4 cup yogurt

1/3 cup milk (coconut milk preferred)

Directions

Blend all the ingredients well until smooth and garnish with coconut scrape or orange zest.

Yogy-fruity smoothie

Servings- 5, Durations- 15minutes

Ingredients

2 cups fat free milk

8 ozs low-fat vanilla yogurt

½ cup thawed pineapple orange juice concentrate

2 cups frozen strawberries

1 banana (coarsely chopped)

Directions

Combine all ingredients and process it well and serve immediately.

Healthy fruity oats smoothie

Servings- 2, Duration- 5minutes

Ingredients

1 banana

1/2 cup strawberries

1/4 cup blueberries

1/2 cup Greek yogurt

1/4 cup oats

1/2 cup orange juice (fresh-squeezed, about 1 orange)

1/2 cup milk

Directions

Puree all the ingredients in the blender and blend until smooth. Serve immediately.

Peachy mango smoothie

Servings- 2, Duration- 10minutes

Ingredients

2/3 cup peaches (frozen sliced)

2/3 cup mango (frozen)

2/3 cup peach nectar

1 tbsp honey

6 ozs fat free yogurt (organic peach)

Directions

Combine all the ingredients and blend it until smooth and serve.

Fruit Smoothies

Tropical fruity cilantro smoothie

Serving-1, Durations- 10minutes

Ingredients

1 cup cilantro (rinsed)

1 cup pineapple (cubed, chilled)

1 banana (sliced)

1 cup orange juice (cold)

Directions

Place all the ingredients in a blender and blend until smooth. Serve Immediately.

Super mango honey smoothie

Servings- 2, Duration -2minutes

Ingredients

1 cup ripe mango

3/4 cup ripe bananas

2/3 cup fat free milk

1 tbsp non-fat dry milk (optional)

1 tsp honey

1/4 tsp vanilla extract

Directions

First- arrange the mango piece and freeze it for an hour and then blend all the ingredients with the frozen mango and serve chilled.

Chocky banana smoothie

Servings- 4, Duration-10minutes

Ingredients

8 ozs soy milk, milk, or coconut milk

1 tbsp honey

2 bananas (frozen)

1 tbsp cocoa powder

Directions

Blend all the above ingredients until smooth and serve chilled.

Gingery peach smoothie

Servings- 4, Duration- 15minutes

Ingredients

1 cup milk

1 peach

1 frozen banana

1 tsp honey

1 dash ginger

1 dash nutmeg

Directions

Puree milk, peach and banana until combined well and taste, if needed add honey. Blend it again by adding ginger and serve immediately by sprinkling nutmeg.

Banana cherry smoothie

Servings- 4, Duration-15minutes

Ingredients

2 cups milk

2 frozen bananas

11/2 cups frozen cherries

2 tsp honey (if needed)

Directions

Blend all the ingredients until smooth. Add honey only if necessary to adjust the sweetness. Serve chilled immediately.

Appy fruity smoothie

Servings- 2, Duration- 5minutes

Ingredients

1 frozen banana

1/2 cup orange juice

1 chopped gala apples

1/4 cup milk

Directions

Add all the ingredients in a blender and blend it until smooth and serve immediately.

Fruity nutty smoothie

Servings- 2, Duration- 5minutes

Ingredients

3 cups almond milk

1 banana

1/2 tsp nutmeg

1 tsp almond extract

2 dates

Directions

Combine all ingredients and blend well in a blender until smooth and serve chilled.

Gold nectar smoothie

Servings- 4, Duration- 15minutes

Ingredients

2 cups orange juice

1/4 cup honey

1 tbsp lemon juice

2 tsp fresh grated ginger

2 ripe bananas

Directions

Place all the above ingredients and puree until smooth and serve.

Creamy peachy smoothie

Servings- 1, Duration-5 minutes

Ingredients

1 cup plain whole milk

1 cup frozen peaches

2 tsp maple syrup

1/2 tsp fresh grated ginger

Directions

Combine well all the ingredients in blender and blend until smooth and serve chilled.

Mango papaya smoothie

Servings- 4, Duration- 15minutes

Ingredients

2 large ripe papayas

1 ripe mango

1 orange

3/4 cup coconut milk

1/2 cup milk (regular)

1 tbsp honey

Directions

Remove the seeds of papaya and add the chopped papaya, mango and orange and then cover it by adding coconut milk, regular milk and tsp honey and blend it until smooth and serve chilled.

Vegetable Smoothies

Cucumber strawberry smoothie

Servings- 2, Duration-15minutes

Ingredients

11/2 cups frozen strawberries

1 cup almond milk (cold)

Cucumber (chopped and deseeded)

2 tsp honey

Lemon

Directions

Combine all the ingredients and blend it well and serve chilled.

Bloody mary spicy smoothie

Servings- 3, Duration- 10minutes

Ingredients

13/4 cups low sodium tomato juice (chilled)

2 tsp fresh lemon juice

1/2 cup English cucumber

2 tsp Worcestershire sauce

3/4 tsp Sriracha (hot Chile sauce)

5 ice cubes

Directions

Take a blender and blend all ingredients until smooth and serve chilled.

Pumpkin low-carb smoothie

Servings- 4, Duration- 15minutes

Ingredients

6 ozs almond milk (unsweetened)

2 ozs heavy cream

1/4 cup pumpkin purée

2 tsp sugar if necessary

1/4 tsp pumpkin pie spice

Directions

Blend all the above ingredients in a blender until smooth and serve immediately.

Purple smoothie

Servings- 4, Duration-15minutes

Ingredients

1cup Red cabbage

1/2 beetroots

1 cup strawberries

1 cup blueberries

1 banana

1/2 apples

2 tsp flaxseed oil

2 cups water

Directions

Place all the ingredients in a blender and blend it well together until smooth. Serve immediately.

Spring smoothie

Servings- 1, Duration- 10minutes

Ingredients

1 cup chilled green tea

1 cup cilantro

1 cup kale

1 cup cucumber

1 cup pineapple

1 lemon

1 tbsp fresh ginger (grated)

1/2 avocado

Directions

Combine the ingredients and blend it well. Serve chilled immediately.

Superbly soy smoothie

Servings- 2, Duration -15minutes

Ingredients

1/2 cup pineapple

1/2 bananas

1/2 cup frozen raspberries

1 tbsp honey

1/4 cup carrot juice

1/2 cup vanilla soy milk

1/2 cup fresh orange juice

Directions

Place all the ingredients in a blender and blend it well until smooth and serve immediately.

Golden carrot smoothie

Serving- 4, Durations- 5minutes

Ingredients

3 cups frozen mango

2 cups carrots

1 orange

1 cup water

Directions

Blend all the ingredients and serve it chilled immediately.

Spicy pumpkin smoothie

Servings- 2, Duration -15minutes

Ingredients

1 cup low-fat vanilla yogurt

3/4 cup chilled pumpkin

1/2 cup ice cubes

1/3 cup fresh orange juice

1 tbsp brown sugar

1/2 tsp ground cinnamon

1/8 tsp ground nutmeg

1 dash ground cloves

1 ripe banana

1 dash ground cinnamon (optional)

Directions

Blend all the above ingredients well in a blender and serve immediately.

Harvest smoothie

Servings- 1, Duration – 60minutes

Ingredients

1 cup almond milk

1/4 cup rolled oats

1 tbsp Chia seeds

1/2 cup pumpkin

1 tbsp blackstrap molasses

1 frozen banana

1 tsp cinnamon

1/2 tsp ginger

1 pinch nutmeg

Ice (if desired)

Directions

Try to soak the Chia seeds, Oats in almond milk for an hour. Add all ingredients into blender and blend until smooth. Add ice if desired.

Pumpkin pie smoothie

Servings- 4, Duration- 2minutes

Ingredients

15 ozs pumpkin purée

12 frozen apple juice concentrate

1/8 tsp ground nutmeg

1 tsp ground cinnamon

21/2 cups water

Directions

Combine all the ingredients and blend it until smooth and serve chilled.

Super food Smoothies

Lemonade Aloe Vera smoothie

Servings- 2, Duration- 10minutes

Ingredients

1 cup water

1/2 avocado

1 medium aloe vera leaf or ½ cup aloe vera gel

1/2 medium lemon, peeled and deseeded

1/2 medium lime, peeled and deseeded

1 tablespoon coconut oil

A dash of Celtic sea salt

1 tablespoon honey

4 – 6 ice cubes

Directions

Combine all the ingredients into until nice and smooth and Serve chilled immediately.

Bee Pollen Blissful smoothie

Servings- 2, Duration – 5minutes

Ingredients

1 cup milk

1 cup frozen blueberries

1/2 fresh or frozen medium banana

1 tablespoon bee pollen

1 tablespoon coconut oil

A little honey

Directions

Combine all ingredients in a blender and blend well till a smoothie texture and serve immediately.

Gingerly Butter chocolate smoothie

Servings- 4, Duration – 10 minutes

Ingredients

1 cup of warm to hot tea

1 tablespoon grass-fed butter

1 tablespoon Chia seeds or Chia seed gel

1/2 tablespoon cacao powder

3/4 teaspoon powdered ginger

1/4 teaspoon cayenne pepper

1/4 teaspoon vanilla extract or powder

1/4 teaspoon cinnamon

2 teaspoons honey

Directions

Place all the above ingredients in a blender and blend it until smooth and serve immediately.

Chlorella Pineapple smoothie

Servings- 2, Duration – 8 minutes

Ingredients

1 cup coconut water

1/2 cup fresh or frozen pineapple chunks

1/3 small avocado

1/4 cup yogurt (preferably full-fat variety)

4-6 fresh basil leaves

1 teaspoon chlorella

1 teaspoon Chia seeds or Chia seed gel

1 teaspoon maca

1 teaspoon bee pollen

Squeeze of lemon juice

A dash of sea salt

A little honey

Directions

Take a blender and place all the above ingredients and blend until smooth and serve immediately.

Super energizer coconut smoothie

Servings- 2, Duration- 5 minutes

Ingredients

1 cup coconut water

1/2 avocado

1/2 cup tropical fruit (pineapple, mango, papaya or a combo)

1/2 cup spinach

1/2 cup kale

1/3 cup Greek yogurt

2 tablespoons goji berries

2 tablespoons dried cranberries

1 tablespoon coconut flakes

1 teaspoon coconut oil

1 teaspoon maca

1 teaspoon wheatgrass powder

A little honey

Directions

Place all the above ingredients in a super fats blender and blend it until smooth, serve and enjoy!!!!

Gelatin T-mac smoothie

Servings- 2, Duration- 10minutes

Ingredients

1 cup water

1/2 cup frozen dark sweet cherries

1/2 cup frozen blueberries

1 tablespoon gelatin

1 tablespoon chia seeds or chia seed gel

1 tablespoon coconut oil

A dash of sea salt

Directions

Place the ingredients in the blender and blend well until smooth and serve immediately.

Goji-Raspy smoothie

Servings- 4, Duration- 10minutes

Ingredients

1 cup milk of your choice

1 cup fresh or frozen raspberries

2 tablespoons goji berries

1/2 tablespoon coconut oil

1/2 tablespoon bee pollen

A little honey

Directions

Combine well all the ingredients and place it in the blender and blend well. Serve immediately.

Hemp brain booster smoothie

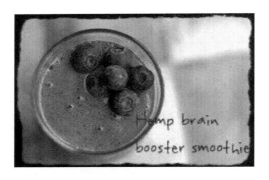

Servings- 2, Duration- 5minutes

Ingredients

1 cup apple juice

1/2 cup frozen blueberries

1/2 fresh or frozen medium banana

2 tablespoons goji berries

2 tablespoons hemp seeds

1 teaspoon coconut oil

Directions

Place all the ingredients in a blender and blend well until smooth and serve immediately.

Marvelous maca smoothie

Servings- 2, Duration- 5minutes

Ingredients

1 cup of warm tea

1 heaping tablespoon chia seeds or chia seed gel

1 tablespoon coconut oil

1 tablespoon maca

1/2 tablespoon cacao powder

A dash of salt

1/2 tablespoon raw honey

Directions

Blend all the ingredients in a blender and serve immediately for a healthy drink.

Colostrums chocolate smoothie

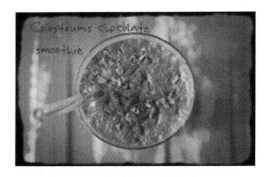

Servings- 2, Duration- 10minutes

Ingredients

1 cup of warm to hot tea

1 heaping tablespoon coconut oil

1 heaping tablespoon chia seeds or chia seed gel

1 tablespoon colostrums

1/2 tablespoon cacao powder

A dash of sea salt

1/2 tablespoon raw honey or maple syrup

Directions

Place all the above ingredients in a blender and blend well until smooth and serve and enjoy!!!

Nuts & Seeds Smoothies

Chunky monkey smoothie

Servings- 2, Duration- 5minutes

Ingredients

1 cup almond milk

1 frozen medium banana

1 tablespoon almond butter

1 tablespoon cacao powder

1 serving chocolate protein powder (optional)

A little honey

Directions

Combine all the ingredients and blend well until smooth and serve immediately.

Almond berry butter smoothie

Servings- 2, Durations- 10minutes

Ingredients

1 cup almond milk

1/4 cup fresh or frozen blueberries

1/4 cup fresh or frozen raspberries

1/4 cup soaked almonds

1 tablespoon grass-fed butter

1 tablespoon cacao powder

1/4 teaspoon cinnamon

1/4 teaspoon vanilla powder or extract

1 tablespoon honey

Directions

Place all the ingredients in the blender and blend until smooth and serve.

Berry dream chocolate smoothie

Servings- 2, Duration- 10minutes

Ingredients

1 cup almond milk

1/2 cup yogurt

1/2 small avocado

1/2 cup fresh or frozen blueberries

3 Brazil nuts

1 tablespoon cacao powder

1 teaspoon cacao nibs

1 teaspoon maca

1 teaspoon lucuma

1/4 teaspoon cinnamon

2 drops vanilla extract

Directions

Combine all the ingredients in a blender and blend until smooth and serve immediately.

Cashew carrot cake smoothie

Servings- 4, Duration- 10minutes

Ingredients

1 cup water

1 cup carrots, washed and chopped

1/2 medium avocado

1/4 cup soaked cashews

1 teaspoon coconut oil

Juice of 1/4 lemon

1/4 inch chopped ginger or ginger powder

1/2 teaspoon cinnamon

1/4 teaspoon ground nutmeg

1 tablespoon honey to sweeten

Directions

Combine all in a blender and blend well until smooth and serve the rich smoothie.

Suppressing chia seed smoothie

Servings- 2, Duration-5minutes

Ingredients

1 cup green tea

1/3 medium avocado

1 kiwi, skin removed

1 cup baby spinach

1/2 cup fresh or frozen blueberries

1 tablespoon chia seeds or chia seed gel

1/2 teaspoon turmeric

1/2 teaspoon ginger

1/4 teaspoon cinnamon

1/2 tablespoon honey

Directions

Place all the ingredients in a blender and blend until smoothie consistency and serve immediately.

Flaxy red-hot fruit smoothie

Servings- 2, Duration- 5minutes

Ingredients

1 cup water

1/2 avocado or a banana

1/2 cup fresh or frozen strawberries

1 tablespoon flax seeds

1/4 teaspoon cayenne pepper

1 tablespoon honey

Directions

Run a blender by adding all the above ingredients to a smoothie consistency and serve immediately to enjoy a healthy drink.

Macadamia nuts coconut smoothie

Servings-2, Duration- 5minutes

Ingredients

1 cup coconut water

1/4 of an avocado

1/2 fresh or frozen banana

6 macadamia nuts

1 tablespoon coconut flakes or shreds

1/2 teaspoon cinnamon

A little honey

Directions

Place all the ingredients in a blender and blend well until smooth and serve immediately.

Peanut butter blast smoothie

Servings- 2, Duration- 5minutes

Ingredients

1 cup yogurt

1 fresh or frozen banana

1/2 cup fresh or frozen raspberries

2 tablespoons peanut butter

1 tablespoon cacao powder

Directions

Place all the ingredients in a blender and blend until smooth and serve chilled.

Spirulina berry smoothie

Servings-2, Duration- 5minutes

Ingredients

1 cup almond milk

1/3 avocado

1/2 cup fresh or frozen blueberries

1 tablespoon tahini

1 tablespoon cacao powder

1/2 tablespoon cacao nibs

1/2 tablespoon spirulina

1/4 teaspoon vanilla powder or extract

1/2 tablespoon honey to sweeten

Directions

Place all the ingredients in the blender and blend until smooth and serve immediately.

Oat berry smoothie

Servings- 2, Duration- 5minutes

Ingredients

35 grams rolled oats

170 grams fat free Greek yogurt

120 grams frozen blueberries

120 ml water

1 bananas (frozen)

Directions

Blend all the ingredients in a blender and serve immediately in glasses.

Herbs & Spices Smoothies

Basil green berry smoothie

Servings- 2, Duration-5minutes

Ingredients

1 cup water

1 fresh or frozen medium banana

1 cup baby spinach

6-8 fresh basil leaves

1 cup fresh or frozen berries

1 tablespoon coconut oil

1/4 teaspoon cinnamon

A little honey

Directions

Blend all the above ingredients together in a blender until smooth and serve chilled.

Spicy green spinach smoothie

Servings-2, Duration- 5minutes

Ingredients

1 cup water

1 cup baby spinach

1 fresh or frozen medium banana

1/2 tablespoon coconut oil

1/4 teaspoon cayenne pepper and/or chili powder

A little honey

Directions

Place all the above ingredients in a blender and blend until smooth and serve immediately.

Hot & spicy green smoothie

Servings- 2, Duration- 5minutes

Ingredients

1 cup water

1/2 medium avocado

1 cup baby spinach

1/2 cup fresh or frozen blueberries

1 tablespoon chia seeds or chia seed gel

1/2 tablespoon coconut oil

1/4 teaspoon chili powder

1/2 tablespoon honey

Directions

Blend all the ingredients into a smooth mixture and serve chilled immediately.

Cilantro smoothie

Servings- 2, Duration- 5minutes

Ingredients

1 cup water

3 ice cubes

1 fresh or frozen medium banana

1/2 cup cilantro

Juice of 1/2 lime

1/2 tablespoon coconut oil

A dash of sea salt

A little honey

Directions

Blend all the ingredients listed and serve it in a glass immediately.

Ultimate turmeric fruity smoothie

Servings- 2, Duration- 5minutes

Ingredients

1 cup water

1 small apple

1/3 fresh or frozen banana

5 fresh or frozen blackberries

2 fresh or frozen strawberries

1/3 cup bilberries

5 soaked almonds

1 tablespoon soaked oats

1 tablespoon macadamia nut oil

1 teaspoon turmeric

1/4 inch ginger

1/2 teaspoon cinnamon

Directions

Blend all the ingredients in a blender until smoothie consistency and serve immediately.

Beet- fruity smoothie

Servings- 2, Duration- 5minutes

Ingredients

1 cup water

1/2 cup beet greens

1/2 cup cooked beets

1/2 cup frozen blackberries

1/2 cup frozen raspberries

1/2 medium lemon, peeled and deseeded

1 tablespoon coconut oil

1/4 inch ginger

Directions

Place all the ingredients in the blender until smooth and serve immediately.

Chocó-minty smoothie

Servings-2, Durations- 10minutes

Ingredients

1 cup milk

1/2 avocado

1 tablespoon cacao nibs

1 serving chocolate protein powder

1 handful of fresh mint leaves

A little honey

Directions

Place all the ingredients in a blender and blend on high for 30-45 seconds until nice and smooth.

Day dream smoothie

Servings- 2, Durations- 5minutes

Ingredients

1/2 cup warm milk

1/2 fresh medium banana

1/2 cup pitted cherries

1/4 teaspoon nutmeg

1 teaspoon honey

Directions

Combine all the ingredients in a blender until smoothie and serve immediately.

Rosemary greenly smoothie

Servings-2, Durations- 5minutes

Ingredients

1 cup water

1 fresh medium banana

1 cup frozen blueberries

1 cup baby spinach

1 sprig fresh rosemary

A dash of high quality salt

A little honey

Directions

Place all the ingredients in the blender until smooth and serve immediately.

Savory sage smoothie

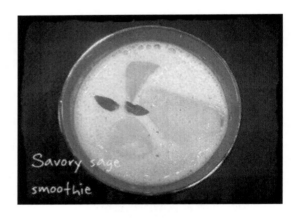

Servings- 2, Durations- 5minutes

Ingredients

1 cup milk of your choice

1 fresh or frozen medium banana

2-4 fresh sage leaves, roughly chopped

1/4 teaspoon cinnamon

A little honey

2-4 ice cubes

Directions

Place all the ingredients in the blender until smooth and serve immediately.

Conclusion

I hope this book gave you some useful insights on what is DASH diet, what are its guidelines and how it can help you lower your blood pressure and reduce your weight. I am sure you'll find the smoothie recipes in this book easy to prepare and delicious to drink.

Please remember that this is not a crash diet that you can follow for a week, shed a few pounds and go back to your old diet habits. Your goal should be to make DASH diet a lifelong habit. Ensure that you consume at least one glass of healthy smoothie every day. This would help you to stay healthy and enjoy the benefits of the diet in the long run. This is not just for people with hypertension. The entire family can follow this healthy diet plan as it is easy and safe to follow. Consulting your doctor before starting the diet is highly recommended.

Thank you!

Thank you for buying and downloading my book DASH Diet Smoothies! Finally, if you enjoyed this book, please take the time to share your thoughts and post a review on Amazon. It'd be greatly appreciated!

This feedback will help me to continue writing the kind of books that would give you the maximum value and results. Thank you once again and good luck!

Don't forget to claim your free bonus here: http://dietcookbooks.co/dashdiet/

FREE BONUS!

To help you start your DASH diet and stay committed to your diet plan, I've put together a DASH Diet Hamper which includes the following:

a. Audio version of the Amazon Bestseller book **"Blood Pressure Solution" by Jessica Robbins**
b. **7 day vegetarian meal plan** for DASH Diet
c. Tips to reduce sodium
d. DASH Diet Shopping List
e. Tips to get started with the DASH Diet
f. Sodium Content Chart of various foods

Additional Bonus!

Receive the first copies of all my diet and cookbooks as soon as they get published for FREE!

Get Access to the FREE DASH Diet Hamper HERE:
http://dietcookbooks.co/dashdiet/

Recommended Reading

I highly recommend you to read some of these other great resources on DASH Diet & Smoothie Recipes:

360 Days of Smoothie Recipes by Emma Katie

Nuribullet Recipe Book by Stephanie Shaw

The Smoothie Recipe Book

365 Days of Juicing Recipes by Emma Katie

DASH Diet for Vegetarians by Renee Sanders

The DASH Diet Weight Loss Solution by Marla Keller

The Everyday DASH Diet Cookbook by Marla Keller

The DASH Diet Action Plan by Marla Keller

DASH Diet Slow Cooker Recipes by Maddie Bridges

The DASH Diet for Beginners by Gina Crawford

Disclaimer

This eBook, DASH Diet Smoothies is written with an intention to serve as a purely informational and educational resource. It is not intended to be a medical advice or a medical guide. Although proper care has been taken to ensure the validity and reliability of the information provided in this eBook, readers are advised to exert caution before using any of the information, suggestions, and methods described in this book.

The writer does not advocate the use of any of the suggestions, diets, and health programs mentioned in this book. This book is not intended to take the place of a medical professional, a doctor and physician. The information in this book should not be used without the explicit advice from medically trained professionals especially in cases where urgent diagnosis and medical treatment is required. The author or publisher cannot be held responsible for any personal or commercial damage in misinterpreting or misunderstanding any part of the book.

Made in the USA
San Bernardino, CA
11 January 2017